THE 4 VITAL PRINCIPLES OF BUSINESS SUCCESS

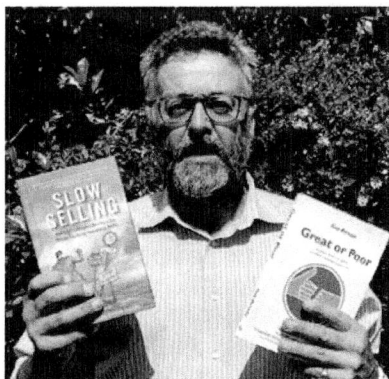

GUY ARNOLD

Guy Arnold is a philanthropist working with small businesses across the UK: his mission is to help them survive and thrive, no matter how vicious their competition, through applying 4 simple, powerful principles, step by step in all they do.

He is the founder of the not-for-profit organisations 'Slow Selling' and 'Investors in Feedback.'

He has worked as a close advisor to hundreds of businesses, large and small over two decades, has run businesses that have won multiple national awards, and also businesses that have struggled to survive.

CONTENTS

THE 4 VITAL PRINCIPLES OF BUSINESS SUCCESS

INTRODUCTION

Hello, and welcome to 'THE 4 VITAL PRINCIPLES OF BUSINESS SUCCESS.'

My name's Guy Arnold and I'm the founder of 'Slow Selling'.

These are the four key principles at the heart of Slow Selling, the heart of my book 'Great or Poor,' and of course, 'Slow Selling.' These, I believe, are the secret principles and systems of the world's most successful businesses.

So thank you for joining me. Well done for taking the time – and I mean that sincerely. Life's so busy. It's so hard to stop and actually do these sorts of things. Everyone's trying to sell you something. Everyone's trying to get your attention. So thank you and well done for taking the time to slow down and spend a bit of time on this material - because it's really very, very difficult out there.

As Einstein said, the definition of insanity is *"Doing the same thing over and over again and expecting different results."* So what I really advise you to do is have a notepad with you and write a 'could do' list. This is just going to be a list of all the ideas that you find in this presentation; all the ideas that you think, "Oh, I might be able to do that. I could do that." At the end of it you can go through it, filter it out, and pick on two or three that you are actually going to do.

So get a pen and paper and actually take some notes and make some action - because that's the key to this.

So why am I here, and how did this come about?

Well, my background is in pubs and hotels. I spent a long career working for myself and other businesses, and my specialism was turning around bankrupt businesses. That's where I got started.

I then bought a bankrupt business, turned it around and sold it on, and then I worked for a big pub company - (well, a small pub company when I joined them) - first as an Area Manager, then as a Regional Director, and then as a Field Operations Director responsible for thousands and thousands of independent pub businesses.

The key there was I noticed that some people were able to take on terrible pubs, turn them around and make them special, whereas other people would take on fantastic operations, and mess them up. So what was the difference?

Those who could take on the poor businesses and make them into great successes, what did they do differently? How did they act? What system did they use? What principles did they follow? What actions did they take?

Trying to answer that question became an obsession for me both as an Area Manager, Regional Director, and as the Field Operations Director, because I felt that if I could find the answer to that question, we could then turn that into training and support for all these people and help them make great successes of their businesses.

If you can learn what the successful people do, and then teach it, and put the systems in place to help people actually take action, they will be able to replicate the success little by little, step by step in their businesses.

That is the foundation of all of this work, which culminated in 2012 with me publishing my first book – **'Great or Poor.'** You can find that and download it from my website, or you can get it from any reputable book-selling website.

I've published another couple of books, but my final book on this subject is one called 'Slow Selling.' This is what these 4 principles are all about: the ability for business owners to slow down, focus on principles at work, and then put them into practice, step by step in your business.

So that's what it's all about. That's why I'm here, and you will find all sorts of free resources on my website.

I am doing this on a not-for-profit basis, so please don't ever feel that I'm trying to sell you something or there's a hidden agenda here. There absolutely isn't! The whole point of this is to try and help people who are running their own businesses.

So why is that?

Well, every year in the UK between four and five million new businesses start up. Yet after three years, about 60 per cent of those will have failed, and after ten years, almost 80 per cent of businesses will fail.

So within three years, almost two thirds of businesses fail and within ten years, almost four fifths of all businesses fail.

Those that don't fail – (the ones that are left) - so many studies show that those who run their own businesses, over 80 per cent of them say that they're either quite stressed, or very stressed all the time, trying to make ends meet, trying to find new customers, trying to compete in a difficult market, trying to stand out, trying to do all this without getting super stressed and feeling frazzled all the time.

So it's a really tough market for small businesses.

Yet there are a few simple principles that make all the difference and these are what we will teach you in this short book.

Now the problem is, of course, everyone else out there is just trying to sell you stuff. They want to sell you marketing, they want to sell you a website, they want to sell you social media promotions, they want to sell you email systems, they want to sell you all sorts of stuff in order to say:

- "Boost yourself. Develop your business, get in front of customers, do this sort of stuff, shout more, give more offers."

Everyone is going to be promoting that to you because that's how they make money.

And of course, there is a little bit of value in those things but it really isn't the answer - because the one thing that small businesses can do so much better than their bigger competition <u>is that they can have more loyal customers and a better reputation</u>.

Everyone says, **"We need to get loyal customers and we need to build a reputation."** But how do you do that? Nobody up to now has said to you, "This is how you do it!"

When I was at this pub company, many people tried to come and sell us training courses. I would say to them, "That's fantastic! What I propose is we pay you on results. If you train our people on customer service, customer loyalty, customer reputation, that's great! We'll pay you on results. We'll pay you twice as much if you get the results you say you can do."

Unfortunately, not one of them called my bluff and went for this … so we did our own research and designed our own support systems.

You can take a horse to water but you can't make it drink! You can train people, but you can't make them do it. You can say 'give good customer service', but you can't make them do it.

The point behind this is that everybody knows this stuff is important, but nobody's selling it, no one's promoting it, no one's giving a proper thought through, methodical, systematic, step by step process that enables you to deliver it.

Whether you're working on your own, or whether you're working with a team of people doesn't matter. To deliver it consistently and continually every day that's the thing that really matters.

So no one's out there trying to sell you this stuff, (because there's very little money trying to sell you this stuff). They all want to sell you marketing and promotions and all that old stuff. But actually, you know, it's common bloody sense that this is the key to independent businesses. This is the one thing that you can do better than anyone else.

Now the first thing just to mention before we get off this introductory part is just to say to you how easy is it to change your habits?

There's going to be a whole lot of stuff that we're going to be talking about here.

But how easy is it to change?

Of course, you'll say to me the answer is, *"It's bloody hard to change"*. I know that it's a good idea to develop a habit of going to the gym, eating healthily and getting a good night's sleep, but it's bloody hard to do it," and everything that is worthwhile, everything that gives great long term results, is the same.

- We all know what we need to do to be fit and healthy, but it's hard to do it.

- We all know what we need to do in order to be intelligent, but it's hard to do it.

- We all know what we need to do to be more effective, but it's hard to do it!

So, in order to change your habits, I would like to point you to two pieces of work that really will help, and work on this area – and we can train you and help you with these two pieces of material as well.

The first piece of work is called 'The 7 Habits of Highly Effective People.' This was published in 1984 and has now sold almost 50 million copies around the world. It is absolutely recognised as the most effective, the most influential, personal improvement material in the world. So have a look at that. There's loads of free resources on the web, particularly on YouTube.' There are groups that meet up and there's training available.

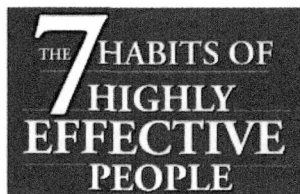

The second is a book that's relatively recently published called 'Atomic Habits' by James Clear. This is really worth a listen, or a read, because it's about how do you change your habits in small steps?

As I say, hopefully you're going to end up with a big 'could do' list and there's going to be loads of things you can say, "I want to change that, I want to change that, I want to change that," but the difficult thing is to actually change things.

So there you are. That's the introduction. We now move on to a few ideas and principles of what do you want to solve, and how are you going to solve them?

WHAT DO YOU WANT TO SOLVE?

The next step in the '4 Vital Principles of Business Success' is what do you want to solve?

In our live training courses on this we get people to write a big list of what the issues are. I'm guessing that the some of the issues are:

- How can I find more customers more easily?
- How can I charge enough for my services?
- If things are going wrong, how can I go back to customers and renegotiate the deal?
- How can I compete against bigger competition?
- How can I compete when I'm being undercut on price?
- How can I be more visible?
- How can I be more organised?
- How can I get more referrals?
- How can I build a better reputation?
- How can I just work on my business when I'm so busy working in it?

There may be a whole load of stuff around that and I'm sure there is. These 4 principles will answer all of those issues. And if you have any specific questions, please do feel free to contact us. It is Support@Slow-Selling.org. Please do feel free to contact us. We always reply to every email that we receive. Sometimes it takes a short while, but we always reply.

There are also lots of free downloads on our website: www.Slow-Selling.org. There are free handouts there, there's free information there, and everything we refer to in this presentation will be available to download there for free. click on the tab that says 'Resources' and you'll find all of the free stuff there.

There'll also be places to sign up for the 'Starter 4 10' or sign up to our mailing list. You can do that as well. There's no obligation. It's up to you, but if you like what we're saying and you want to start integrating it into your business, I do strongly recommend the 'Slow Selling Starter 4 10' because that absolutely gets you started. It's incredibly cheap – (costs you next to nothing) - and gets you started step by step. You'll get one tip every day for the next seven weeks that you can integrate into your business in just 10 minutes a day. And that really gets you going!

www.starter410.org

So there you are! Without further ado, let's get into the material. Let's talk about the principles, and then let's talk about how you can move forward.

THE 4 VITAL PRINCIPLES OF BUSINESS SUCCESS AND THE SLOW SELLING MOVEMENT

As we already discussed: a huge percentage of small businesses fail every every year, and the people who survive say that they are generally either stressed or very stressed.

The key thing here is that you might be excellent at what you do - I'm sure you are excellent at what you do, and I'm sure you're also an interesting and motivated person otherwise you wouldn't be reading this - **but doing what you do and running a business doing what you do, are completely different skills.**

So this is all about how to run a business doing what you do.

This is about principles - and principles are like lighthouses – they don't change.

Principles just show you what is the right direction and what is the right thing to do. Otherwise, you're like a ship at sea with no rudder, no compass, and of course you're going to be with the 80 per cent who end up on the rocks.

So it's really important to learn these principles and then start applying them step by step. We will teach you how to do this step by step. Don't worry about anything! Don't worry about information overload. Just keep making your 'could do' list, and we will show you how to apply this step by step in your business.

So here are some issues that you're probably aware of:

1. **Everyone knows it's a great idea to deliver good customer service.** Everyone bloody tells you, but the real question is **how on earth do you actually do that**? How do you get time to do it yourself if you're on your own? How do you make sure that everyone you employ does it, or people who perhaps you subcontract to? How do you actually make sure that happens? So often you know as a customer, it doesn't.

2. **The internet empowers your customer to spread the word about you at the speed of light.** Well, that's really good news if you're delivering a consistent and continuing-improving customer experience. But what if you're letting people down? What if just one person lets people down? What if you just have one link in your chain that lets people down? What are people going to be spreading the word about you at the speed of light?.

Going back to the previous point where I said everyone knows it's a great idea to deliver good customer service – the other point I want to say there is that actually this isn't about customer service. This is a really, really important point, and definitely something for your 'could do' list. Make a note of this and tell everyone who's involved in your business:

Customer service is about what you think you're doing. The customer doesn't give a damn about what you think you're doing. The customer is only interested in *their* experience.

So, from now on, please never ever use the word 'customer service.' It's completely irrelevant. It doesn't matter. It's only your delusion of what you think you're doing. The only thing that matters is customer experience, and that is judged by what they think you're doing, what their experience is and how they see you.

> Principle:
>
> • 'Customer service' is irrelevant...
>
> •What matters to the customer is their experience!

3. **The customer has unlimited choice** in the world today, so why on earth are they going to choose you? You've got to give them a valid, good reason to choose you. It's got to be both value and excellence, because the competition is mad out there.

4. **It's easy to communicate.** You can write blogs, you can just flood the world with information, but you're shouting into space. It's easy to communicate, but your communication is going to get lost. There's far too much information out there. No one's paying any attention. There's massive noise. It's like trying to hear a whisper in a football crowd.

5. **Competition and change can spring up overnight.** You might be doing okay today, but what about tomorrow? What's happening? What are people developing on the other side of the world that could change the world overnight? Of course, we

know businesses all the time - taxi drivers, bookshops, almost every business, has been changed by the Internet almost overnight. The new thing is AI, which is going to put professional services really under pressure.

So competition and change can spring up overnight. Your business needs to be robust enough so that customers are loyal to you, so that they're telling you what changes are occurring in their life. They're telling you what other things are being offered to them. They're helping you. They're working with you. **They're telling you the things you need to know in order to survive and grow, innovate and change.**

6. **Everybody's busy and stressed**. Everybody's going to try and sell you something. Everybody wants their pound of flesh from you. Who on earth can you turn to? What on earth can you know and do, that you can trust?

That is what we're trying to achieve here with the '4 Vital Principles of Business Success' and the Slow Selling movement.

We're aiming to be an organisation, a set of principles that you can trust.

Not just because we're trustworthy, but because they're bloody obvious common sense! They are unarguable against. They are timeless. They are universal. They are self-evident, common sense.

LOYALTY, REPUTATION & REFERRALS

The next thing to discuss is loyalty, reputation and referrals. We've already mentioned this - and it's bloody obvious common sense that **the best way as a small business to grow is through loyalty, reputation, and referrals.**

Whenever I go into a new company, I explain this to them. That's why they've hired me!

I say to them, "Well, what do your customers actually think of you? What is your reputation? What is your loyalty?" They say, "Well, we *hope* t's quite good." They always say that. They always say, "We *hope* it's quite good." I don't say this - because it will be a rude thing to say – and I'm a very polite person, but I think to myself:

"Hope is *not* a strategy!"

Hope is not a strategy: You have got to be smarter than that. You cannot hope.

Hope is just a recipe for disaster. It's like if you're a finance person, saying to your accountant, "How are my books looking?" and they say,

- "Well, I hope it's okay because the bank hasn't been been ringing and there doesn't seem to be too many bounced cheques."

You've got to be smarter than that. You need to be *absolutely* on top of your loyalty, reputation and referrals. This is your No 1 business driver, and the key is to be *absolutely* on top of it.

This is what we will teach you to do, because it's the most important thing in your business. And there is a way of being on top of it. You don't need to rely on hope anymore. You don't need to keep your fingers crossed. You don't need to listen to endless people saying, "Oh, we want to deliver good customer service." They're just talking bollocks. They don't *know* how to do this. They just spout the same old rubbish.

There is a way of doing this and you're about to learn it.

The other thing that's really important here is that every solution, everything that we tell you, must be simple.

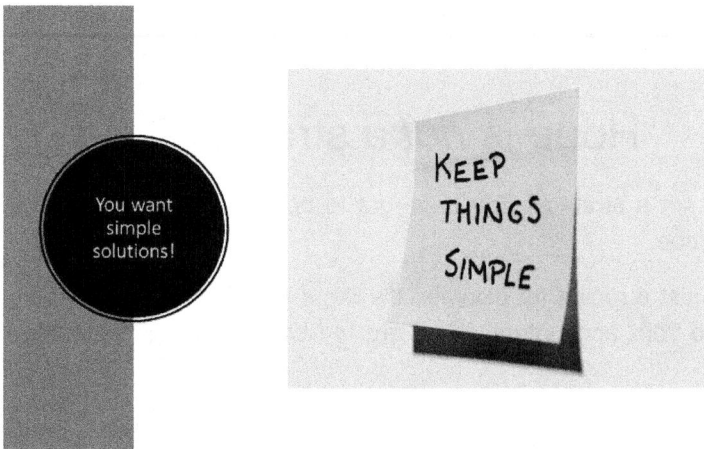

You want simple solutions!

KEEP THINGS SIMPLE

Life's complicated enough. You're running your own business. You're running around chasing your tail. You do not need someone like us giving you complicated "Here are 27 steps to delivering customer loyalty." You don't need that.

You need **really simple four self-evident, universal, common sense principles that you can apply to everything** - and that is exactly what we are going to tell you.

SYSTEMS AND PRINCIPLES

So, taking this forward, what we talked about last time was a whole load of ideas about customer experience rather than customer service. The most important thing is keeping it simple by principles; sound principles.

So everything in this material has three things to it.

1. **It's going to be principle driven.**

   Principles are self-evident, timeless, universal common sense that act like lighthouses and show you the way to go.

2. **They are going to help you build simple systems.**

   We'll talk about simple systems in a minute. Systems are what makes things happen, not hope. So you need simple systems.

3. **Everything can be implemented by you step by step.**

   Step by step is what works. Slow and steady wins the race. The 'aggregation of marginal gains,' to quote the coach of the British cycling team. The continual improvement, step by step, that makes winners in every scope of life.

Principles

Consistency & Continual
Improvement

Step by step

That's exactly what we're going to teach you.

- This is not a flash in the pan.
- This is not a quick fix.
- This is not a "Do these 17 things and you will get customers flooding to you in an avalanche that you can't control."

It's not all that old rubbish. It is principles to drive simple systems, step by step, that you can apply at any stage continually in your business.

So very quickly, do you need systems? You may think, "Well, I'm a small business. I haven't got time for systems. I'm in control. I know what it is."

Well, do you have a system for managing your money? Do you have a system for delivering your goods or services to your customers?

Do you have a system for running your marketing and your advertising?

You probably do. If you don't, I'd be very surprised.

My suggestion to you is that *if* **customer reputation, and loyalty, and referrals are the single most important thing of your business** - and if you're a small business they *have* to be - **then surely it's a great idea to have a system in place to make them work consistently brilliantly.**

Your choice! If you don't want a system, please stop reading.

Systems are going to make this work. These are not complicated systems. They're simple systems that you're going to enjoy putting into place, but they are nevertheless systems. If you're the sort of person who just likes to wing it, and fly by the seat of your pants, then please don't read any further. You're not going to get anywhere with this.

So systems are very important.

PRINCIPLES

We're going to talk now about a few principles, and then we're going to start off getting into the whole idea behind the '4 Vital Principles of Success.'

1. **If you want to achieve something you've never achieved before, you need to do things you've never done before.**

   So remember, your 'could do' list. Keep going back to your 'could do' list and put on there a whole lot of 'could do' things.

2. **Customer service is irrelevant, remember. It's all about customer experience.**

3. **The key to customer experience is 1. Consistency, and 2. Continual improvement.**

How do you get consistency and continual improvement? The answer is, of course, through systems.

The wonderful people to talk about systems – and I'm not suggesting that you should run your business like this, but absolutely the proof of systems is of course McDonald's.

Now are McDonald's the world's greatest hamburger chefs? Absolutely not.

Are they amazing at customer service? Absolutely not.

But they are phenomenally brilliant at consistency and continual improvement in small steps? Yes! Absolutely! How do they do that? They do it through systems.

If you want to read about systems and about obsession on systems and getting it right, there's a wonderful book here. It's a film as well. The book is called 'Grinding it Out' by Ray Kroc. The film is called 'The Founder' which is the same sort of story. It's a bit more Hollywood-ised, but it's the same kind of thing.

Ray Kroc was a milkshake mix salesman who came across the McDonald brothers and found they were selling ten times as many milkshakes as anyone else. He wanted to find out why that was because he could then explain that to his other customers so they'd buy more milkshake.

He was then so impressed by what he saw with the McDonald brothers' business, he eventually persuaded them to sell him the right to franchise the business. And of course, the rest is all history.

But the thing about Ray Kroc was he was **absolutely obsessed by consistency through systems and continual improvement by systems.**

He wasn't really interested whether it was McDonald's or Jumbo jets. It didn't matter. It was consistency and continual improvement through systems - and that's what we're aiming for, through these '4 Vital Principles of Business Success.'

This is a really important point and one where so many businesses in the UK fall down. We just have this sort of slack mentality in the UK, which is why we don't build anything anymore either! We need to put systems in place that make things work. The Germans are brilliant at it, the Japanese are brilliant, etc, etc, so it's about extraordinary systems that make things work.

4. **Beliefs drive actions.** We need to have a set of beliefs in our business that's going to drive the right actions.

5. **You can take a horse to water, but you can't make it drink.**

   You need to have systems step by step in your business that's going to make all the horses involved with your business, thirsty, so they want to be consistent, they want to drive these fantastic customer experiences that's going to create customer loyalty, reputation and referrals – and they want to help you continually improve.

6. **Small steps in the right direction are better than big steps in any other direction.**

Everything we do will be about small steps - and this is definitely one for your 'could do' list, to write this down: Small steps in the right direction are better than big steps in any other direction.

7. **What gets measured gets done**. If you are trying to create consistency, trying to drive small steps, trying to increase customer loyalty, customer reputation and customer referrals, you've got to have some measures in those areas.

We will talk extensively about measures under Principle No 4.

Principle No 4 is to put the right measures in place. So 'what gets measured, gets done', is a principle. If you want to have the right things done, you've got to have measures of the right things.

So there we are. They're the principles and that's the foundational principles of everything that we're going to cover in the '4 Vital Principles of Business Success.'

So to sum up, the key to success is small, simple systems based on principles, driving consistency and continual improvement, step by step, in the key areas of your business.

	Principles
The key to success is:	Consistency & Continual Improvement
SIMPLE SYSTEMS	Step by step

And if that isn't bloody obvious common sense, I don't know what is. That applies whether your business is a tiny startup, or a large multinational, and anything in between. It absolutely is the case.

The key to success is simple systems based on principles, driving consistency and continual improvement, step by step. And that's exactly what we're going to deliver to you here in Slow Selling.

And one thing before we just finish this part, remember the 'boredom of success.' And when I teach this, I show a picture of Mo Farah, the Mobot. The amount of work that a marathon runner has to put in behind the scenes in order to win the marathon.

Unfortunately, we as spectators just see the final race. We don't see the ten years of work that's behind the scenes.

And the same is true for your business!

An overnight success takes ten years to put into place.

To be proficient at something, you've got to put 10,000 hours into it. So you've got to remember that what I call the 'boredom of success' is very, very important. You need to start doing these things even when they don't have immediate results. Just keep doing them, keep doing them, keep doing them.

What will keep you doing them?

Well, small steps, and the systems that we're going to talk about, and the belief that this is the right thing.

These *are* **timeless, universal principles of common sense**, and therefore it's sensible to do them. But do remember the 'boredom of success." The thing that will stop you from actually doing this stuff is to have to keep doing them continually without any short term, quick fix solutions.

The boredom
of success ...

If you want the short term, quick fix, snake oil salesmen, you can see them everywhere.

Just do a Google search for anything like advertising or promotion or anything like that. They'll be queuing up at your door. There's plenty of them.

You need to just accept that **this isn't a quick fix**.

This is a recipe for a long fix, the slow fix, the long term fix, the fix that will make you rich over time, the fix that will reduce your stress, the fix that will enable you to sleep at night because you are doing the right things for the long term that will drive reputation, loyalty and referrals till they come out of your ears.

That is why we call it Slow Selling.

We're now going to talk about the four principles in themselves, and what they actually are, and then we're going to talk about them one by one and how to apply them in your business.

THE '4 VITAL PRINCIPLES OF SUCCESS: HUMAN BEHAVIOUR

So we've talked about a whole load of principles. So what are the '4 Vital Principles of Business Success? What four principles are the key ones that we need to focus on, and we need to plan our systems and our businesses around in order to make sure that we can achieve this fantastic goal of **great levels of customer loyalty, fantastic reputation, driving people towards us and continual referral and recommendation**?

What are the key things?

We have talked about these principles already, so you will recognise each one of the four principles in what we've already discussed. But now it's the time to clarify all of what we've just discussed into the four vital principles, and then we will run through each principle one by one.

In a nutshell, the '4 Vital Principles of Business Success' are the four principles of human behaviour.

How do humans behave? There are four common sense principles that govern all behaviour - because after all, business is just people dealing with people. People make the decisions, people put the policies in place, people answer the phones, people do the work, people do everything.

In this age of AI and computers and automation, this isn't sexy information. This isn't stuff that people are going to be shouting about, but it is blindingly obvious common sense. It is timeless and it is universal. People do everything. The people govern the AI. The people read the stuff generated by AI. So AI isn't going to change anything. The only thing that AI will change is the fact that people will stop believing what they read - because if computers are going to generate everything, then people are going to stop believing it because it's going to get more and more rubbishy, more and more just clicking on the buttons.

So people adapt and they know what's happening, and they can thrive in their environment. So this AI thing that everyone is currently shouting about is just another adaptation - another reason to go back and stick to the time honoured simple, universal, timeless, common sense principles.

So what are the four principles of behaviour?

Well, the four principles of behaviour is that people behave like bears: B-E-A-R-S.

PEOPLE BEHAVE
LIKE BEARS

B stands for Beliefs. People have a set of beliefs.

- So where do beliefs come from? They come from the subconscious. They come from the environment, they come from upbringing, they come from the people you deal with, they come from the media that you and your customers and your people in your business absorb. They come from how people are treated. If you treat people better, they will have better beliefs. They will have better beliefs about you.

So beliefs come from all sorts of factors, and everybody has a unique set of beliefs. Your beliefs are as unique to you as your DNA because everybody has a different set of ingredients that makes those beliefs.

Your beliefs then give you your emotions – the E of the B-E-A-R.

E stands for Emotions. The emotions are how you feel about anything that comes your way, and how you feel about it will of course be driven by your inner beliefs. We'll run through an example in a minute.

Your emotions then cause you to take action:

A stands for Actions: What you do about the situation, and actions will give you R: Results.

R stands for Results. You have no control over the results. You only have control over the actions. The results come automatically.

This is one of the key things we teach when we coach people. You cannot control the outputs, the results. **You can only control the inputs or the actions,** and you can do that by of course changing the inputs and the actions, but also by working on the emotions, E, and the beliefs, B.

So in a nutshell, B-E-A-R. People behave like BEARS.

Beliefs drive emotions. Emotions drive actions. Actions give you results, and your results almost always reinforce your beliefs.

I said I'd give you an example.

- Let's say I am frightened of spiders. I have a belief that spiders are nasty, dangerous, yucky things. If I see a spider, my emotional will be one of fear. My action will be a fight or flight action. "My brain is triggered. I've got to fight or flight," and the result will be I reinforce my fear of spiders.

- So if I could change that belief to "Well, I don't like spiders, but they're not going to harm me." Of course, that's not a very good belief if you live in Australia where there's lots and lots of very poisonous spiders – but anyway, in the UK I don't like spiders but they're not going to harm me. That's my belief. So I need to find a way to deal with them.

- The emotion when I see one, I feel a bit uncomfortable but I'm going to take some action.
- Action is I'm going to deal with the spider. I'm going to gather a cloth and throw it out the door.
- The result is I'm going to feel better about spiders, because I managed to do that and nothing bad happened to me. So that will reinforce that that belief. It's a circle link.

You've got a vicious circle or a virtuous circle, a circle down making things worse, or circle up making things better.

But basically, the four principles are B, E, A,R: Beliefs, Emotions, Actions, Results.

Those are the four key principles that we're going to talk about: The 4 Vital Principles of Business Success that govern everything in your business.

- What are the beliefs in your business, of you, your people and your customers?
- What are the emotions in your business of you, your people and your customers?
- What are the actions in your business of you, your people and your customers?
- What results will determine your long term success? How can you look at those? What are the things that happen? What are the results you want from you? What are the results you want from your people and what are the results you want from your

customers that will then give you the profitability and the sustainability and the lack of stress that, of course, is exactly what you were looking for back where we started?

So B, E, A, R. What are the beliefs, emotions, actions and results?

And when those translate into the business sphere, I change the words.

In the diagram below you'll see it looks a bit like a wheel with a heart with a hub in the middle. In the middle is the hub, the beliefs, the B.

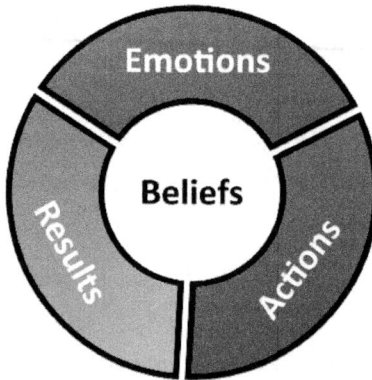

And this is the 4 principles changed the 'The 4 Vital Principles of Business Success'

The 4 Vital Principles of Business Success

For a hub we call it the mission. In fact, we call it the **'Customer Focused Mission,' or CFM for short.** What I'm saying is if you want to have a business that grows predictably, continually and consistently through customer loyalty, reputation, and referrals, you need to start off with a mission to achieve that. This is absolutely vital – because most businesses don't have that mission.

Most businesses have the mission of "I'm here to make money, and also I should treat the customers well." That is absolutely going to kill your business because as soon as stress comes, as soon as problems start occurring, the need to make money will trump the need to treat the customers brilliantly. You will do things that alienate from your customers, that destroy loyalty, destroy reputation.

You don't need me to tell you this. You see it happening with businesses all around you. You start on the downward spiral of disaster, which is why 80 per cent of businesses fail within ten years.

So it's really absolutely critically important to make sure you start off with a belief of **'Our aim in our business is to build customer loyalty, customer reputation, and encourage and incentivise, and make our customers want to refer and recommend us. Our aim is to do the right things so that the money will follow.'**

Not the other way round. Absolutely vital.

Most businesses get this the wrong way around. Most people have it the other way around, which is 'our aim is to make money and also to treat customers well.'

The real answer to this is 'our aim is to treat customers so brilliantly so that we make money.' **Absolutely vital.**

The second one: **E – Emotions**. The emotion is all about the customer's real needs.

Who is the customer? Well, the customer is everyone your business is dealing with, including yourself. So it's yourself, your people, your customers, your community.

What are their real needs? **What are the key *emotional* needs that they need you to fulfil so that they can become fiercely loyal, and spread your reputation for all the right reasons, and want to recommend and refer you?** What emotions do you need to press? What are the key things you need to fulfil so that your customers get those emotions through the experience of your service and your value so that they then take those actions?

It's very important. It sounds complicated, but trust me - bear with this. It actually becomes quite simple because we will simplify this into a few key tools in each principle.

So: First Principle - Customer focused mission: **B**eliefs.

Second Principle - Find the customer's real needs. **E**motions.

Third principle – Actions. The actions we suggest are go the extra inch. The actions of continual improvement in small steps, the aggregation of marginal gains. Small steps in the right direction is so much better than big steps in any other direction. This is the principle of small steps, continuous small steps, using systems.

Remember when we talked about systems. Small steps and systems to continually move forward.

Fourth Principle – Results. Well, what results do we need? We need some measures for our results.

So the fourth principle of the '4 Vital Principles of Business Success' is to have the right measures. To know what we need to measure so that we get the right results,

- so that we stick to our customer focused mission,
- so that we *know* we are fulfilling the customer's real needs.
- And so we find out what we need to *do* to continually go the extra inch, and we measure our progress along those inches so that we can continually move forward.

I hope you're now saying, "Yeah, that's common sense. I get it. That makes sense to me." I'm sure you are. Of course, on all of this, if you have any queries, please contact us. We will put you in touch with the right people or send you the right information that you need to be able to move further forward.

So now, without further ado, we're going to go into each of the four principles one by one.

PRINCIPLE 1: BELIEFS

So here we are! The '4 Vital Principles of Business Success.' Principle number one: Beliefs – The B of B-E-A-R.

The 4 Vital Principles of Business Success

What we're going to suggest here is you need a mission.

You need a **customer focused mission**.

You need something that is going to stop you doing the wrong things in your business because they'll make money today at the expense of making money tomorrow. And so many businesses get this wrong: They focus on money today, yet they don't spend any time and effort working on continual growth, success, profitability, calmness, systems, etc, for continual profitable growth tomorrow because of customer loyalty, reputation, referrals, etc.

So Principle No 1 is slow down and consider your higher purpose.

What do you do? Why do you do it? How could you do it in a way that's going to attract the best people and the most loyal customers?

Let's just consider here a few examples:

- I spent a lot of my career in the pub business.

  What do you do? We sell food and drink. *No!* We do *not* sell food and drink. We give great experiences to people so that they want to rave about us and come back.

  Why do we do it? To make money. *No!* We do *not* do it to make money. We do it so that people think we're so fantastic they come back more often and want to rave about us to our friends.

  How can we do it in a way that will attract the best people and the most loyal customers? We need a mission that keeps us on track.

- How about an insurance company?

  What do we do? We help people make their lives easier and reduce their stress and worry. Why do we do it? Because that's what we're good at, and we enjoy making people feel happier, less stressed and more energised, and taking worries away from them.

- What about an IT company?

  We take the hard work out of being up there and being in the right place in the right way. We just make it easy for people to do the right thing online, not only technically but also on what they actually publish.

So as an IT company we are a one-stop shop that gives the customer peace of mind at sensible prices so that they never have to worry about what's going on in their IT area because we are continually looking at ways to improve, develop and get them saying the right things in the right place in the right way.

Why do we do it? Because that's what we're great at, and we can share that. If we share that brilliantly, then we should make a lot of money.

- Apple. Perfect example. It's not about computers. It's about empowering people to do things that before Apple came along only people with huge amounts of money could do.

- Amazon: What do we do? We aim to be the world's most customer focused company.

- Tesco: what do they do? They earn a customer's lifetime loyalty. Why do they do that? Because that is the only way to be the best in the field, and that's what they are good at. They genuinely believe that. How do they do it: 'Every little helps!'

Have a look at the book 'Management in Ten Words,' by Terry Leahy. It's a fantastic book. I strongly recommend that.

Book Review:
Management in 10 Words
by Sir Terry Leahy

MANAGEMENT IN TEN WORDS TERRY LEAHY

"The perfect read for any business leader looking to find the foundations for a genuine long-term business strategy

This is the introduction from 'Management in 10 Words' by Terry Leahy. He really makes this point very well.

"The room was full of the men and women who run the British government. The question these senior officials asked me was the same one I face time and time again. So how did you do it? What was it that turned Tesco from being a struggling supermarket, No 3 retail chain in the United Kingdom into the third largest retailer in the world?"

"It's quite simple, I said." "We focus relentlessly on delivering for customers. We set ourselves some simple aims and some basic values to live by. We then created a process to achieve them, making sure that everyone knew what they were responsible for."

Silence, polite coughing, someone poured out some water, and more silence. This was the civil service at its most civil. "Was that it?" an official finally asked. The answer to that is, "Yes."

This book is about the lessons I learned as Tesco grew. Some of it that follows may strike you as simple and obvious. Yet I have met and worked with people from different cultures worldwide, have I been struck by how basic simple truths about life - not just business - have been forgotten, or are dismissed as too obvious to matter by clever people who mistake simple for simplistic? We have allowed ourselves to think that because we live in a world which is complicated, the solutions to problems must be complicated as well.

It goes on to be talking about this whole thing about the idea of focusing on customers, earning a customer's loyalty one step at a time, and of course, how do you earn the customers' lifetime loyalty? You will know the answer this if you've ever shopped at Tesco. The answer is 'Every Little Helps."

That's the third principle of the '4 Vital Principles of Business Success': **Go the extra inch. Every Little Helps.**

So that is it. What is your higher purpose? What can you do? Here is your 'could do' list, your thing to do on this principle:

1. **Consider your higher purpose**. List your activities and see how they apply to this purpose. Ask people involved with your business either directly or indirectly, what they think of your business, what motivates them, what do they want for your business? What turns them on?

There was an absolutely wonderful series of adverts many years ago for Carlsberg. Now I think Carlsberg is bloody awful beer, but their advertising was fantastic. They illustrated for example, taxis, and it was outside a nightclub at two in the morning, absolutely pissing down with rain. There's a line of taxis waiting outside the nightclub with all friendly drivers in there having a hot coffee or whatever. The strapline was 'Carlsberg don't do taxis, but if they did…' The point being what is the best? What is the vision of the best possible way of doing this job? The point isn't "Oh, no, we couldn't do that today because we can't cope with that." That doesn't matter. The point is to have this mindset in your mind all the time of 'If we really could nail this, what would it look like?" Then you can move towards that inch by inch using the third principle.

So consider your higher purpose, list your activities and see how they apply to the purpose. Ask your people what motivates them, ask your customers what turns them on, and then distil your ideas and feedback into a customer focused mission.

Those words **'customer focused mission'** are very important. What is a mission? It all sounds very American! What's your mission? Well, our mission is to do this, that, and the other. You've got to get rid of your disbelief here because so many people mess this up. It's where mission is absolutely hugely abused usually by marketing departments.

In so many marketing departments, you see the straplines everywhere: 'Making Things Happen' 'Doing things Brilliantly." It's all marketing bollocks and we do not want that. This is not what we're talking about here.

This is about distilling your ideas - and this word 'distil' is very important because you have all the raw ingredients. They're already there.

What are your beliefs? What are your passions? What do you really want to achieve in life? How do you want to make a difference, (and if you don't want to make a difference and if you don't have this passion, then forget all this because it ain't gonna work for you!) You need to have some sort of passion about how you can make the world a slightly better place by doing what you do, by being so brilliant at what you do.

My passion in doing this is to put as many genuinely valuable resources out there without all the bollocks, without all the polish, because it's so much better just to do it so that you can actually get the right information that you need, as and when you need it.

Please help others by sharing this with them. Send them the information, send them a link, whatever.

So if you haven't got his passion, then forget it.

There needs to be a desire to make life easier.

- If you're an accountant, how can you become this accountant that everybody raves about, and wants to recommend to their friends because you're so helpful, you're so good at answering the phone, you're so accurate, you're so trustworthy, you're on the ball, you're making suggestions to people before they ask questions of you?

That's what you're aiming for. You're not just aiming to be quite a good accountant. You're aiming to be something that is so brilliant that your customers couldn't imagine living without you.

- If you're a cleaning company, cleaning the carpets is normal. We all know that! Everyone expects a clean carpet when you've turned up, but they want you to be fantastically easy to work with. They want you to offer some sort of easy to say yes to service so the carpets just keep clean without them ever having to worry about it. Maybe you want to be a keyholder. You want to be trustworthy. You want to be reliable. You want to be good at reporting. You just want to be the sort of person that people go, "God, we had those carpet cleaners in the other day. They were fantastic! Do you know what they did? They did this, this and this."

This is not about changing the world.

This is about tiny, tiny steps, continually repeated week in, week out, month in, month out, year in, year out so that over time you become this Carlsberg business. Carlsberg don't clean carpets, but if they did... Carlsberg don't do accounts, but if they did....

That sort of idea of **something so wonderful that your customers just wouldn't even consider phoning or contacting anyone else.**

And when you do make mistakes - because you will always make mistakes -, your customers call you and tell you,

- "Hey, Guy, I just need you to know that actually there's a bit of a cock up in that email you sent out the other day." People become your advocates, they become your partners, they become raving fans. Life just gets so much better for both of you!

This is the habit, the principle of vision.

A principle of beginning with the end in mind.

A principle of always aiming for 'win/win' outcomes.

So I'll repeat the 'could do' list again.

- Consider your higher purpose, list your activities and see how they apply to purpose. Ask people what motivates them, or could motivate them. Ask customers what turns them on, or what they don't get that they would love to get? Very, very important there. What don't they get that they would love to get? What's the norm in your industry that's frustrating them or pissing them off, and what would they really like?

If you could wave this magic wand to be this fantastic world class business, even though you're a tiny business, what do they really want from you? To get so close to them to build so much trust that they tell you the absolute truth, and then distilling this stuff into a customer focused mission that gives you a compass driving you forward in everything you do.

It's the compass.

The customer focus mission is the compass. It's the thing you keep looking at to say, "Well, what direction next? What decision next, what system next? Where do I keep going? So your customer focus mission is your compass driving you forward.

I'm going to stop there and we're going to move onto the second principle. If you need more help on customer focus mission, you know who to ask, you know where to come. There's lots and lots and lots of webinars. I've worked with thousands of businesses, helping them put customer focus missions together. Some are better than others, but it's just so important.

I'll just finish with one example.

- I was working with a major bank, one of the big four banks. This is probably about 15 years ago. We were talking about customer focused mission for their commercial arm. We were at their Head Office and we had this meeting where all the top managers were there sitting around this big table. We were going to have a couple of hours on what could be our mission? What is this all about? What is business banking all about? What should we really be focusing on as business banking? It's not about money. It's not about enhancing the services. It's about what do customers really want from a business banker?

- I was warned that one of the people in this group sitting in the corner was going to be really disruptive because he was about to retire in six months time. He was known for being outspoken, and he didn't mind telling everyone exactly what he thought in words of one syllable. So we're having this discussion around the table and lots of ideas. I was at the front. I'd done the training. We then had the discussion and I was flip charting all these ideas. All sorts of exciting things like serving people well and responding and listening and all that sort of stuff. A lull came in the conversation and this bloke said, "This is all crap." I can hear it now! "This is all crap. Surely, business banking is just about long term relationships." And the whole room just went completely silent and everyone said, "Yeah. Yeah, that's it. That's exactly it. That is exactly what it's about." And from then on that was their customer focused mission. *Business banking is all about long term relationships*. Most important things there being **long term**, and **relationship**.

So it's about distilling these ideas, distilling information into a customer focused mission, and getting people to help you do that - because actually it's probably the most difficult thing you can do with your own business.

And I would recommend that you do get someone outside to help you distil this, either someone employed by us, or someone who you trust.

It maybe a friend, maybe a supplier, maybe a group of trusted customers. That would be fantastic, but do get someone to help you and do not land on it until everybody goes, **"Yeah, that's exactly right. That is exactly what we're about."**

PRINCIPLE 2: EMOTIONS

Now we've learnt in Principle No 1 that the first thing to be the BEAR is about your mission, your purpose and what is going to drive you - your compass for everything else.

I like acronyms. So B-E-A-R, Bear. It's easy to remember. You can remember a bear. Customers are like bears. See customers as bears.

BEAR: Beliefs. What's my belief? Oh, yes, I remember we talked about that.

E – Emotions. Ah, you're one of my customers. Ah, I get it, yeah.

The 4 Vital Principles of Business Success

So, I like acronyms, and I use acronyms and easy to remember principles, so that you never need to have a book by your side. You can just remember the stuff, remember the basics, and then apply this stuff, apply the basics, apply the principles step by step through systems, to everything that you do. So hope your 'could do' list is coming on well.

So Principle No 2 is the emotions, the E, and it's about slowing down and considering your customers' emotions at every step of the journey with you. That's a big one.

Slowing down and considering your customers emotions, and we call these **your customers' real needs.**

Now, every customer is unique, every customer is different, and you might say every customer is awkward. I'm sure you wouldn't say that, because I'm sure your customers are lovely – but all customers have different physical needs. Every single customer will have a different physical need from you, and their physical needs might change depending on when they come to you and their environment, and their situation and all that sort of stuff.

But the wonderful thing is that as humans, we all have **similar emotional needs.**

What we're focusing on here is how do we hone this? Let's not worry about each individual customer. Let's look and worry about the likely emotional needs of the customers. The more and more we learn about them at every step of our way, what are the emotions that they are going to want satisfied?

So people take physical actions because of emotional needs.

And again, there's a free resource on this and it's called the customer's real needs is a cup of tea. T-E-A, another lovely acronym for you. Aways remember from from this is the customer's real needs is a cup of tea. Just imagine your customer is sitting down and you're giving them a cup of tea.

THE CUSTOMER'S REAL NEEDS

T stands for Trust.

All customers want to be able to trust you in some way, at some level, because in order to part with their money they want to be able to have some trust that they are making a good decision.

E stands for easier or better life.

All customers want their lives to get easier or better through dealing with you.

Easier life is away from problems and that's the easiest motivator by the way: away from problems. You see all the adverts on telly. 'Dettol kills everything dead'. Get those nasty germs in the toilet. We get them. Let's kill them." Pandemics are really good for Dettol because everyone's frightened and everyone wants to kill everything. Fear is a fantastic motivator! So the E in easier is away from fear, away from problems. That's that's the easiest motivator.

If you want to sell a legal service – let's say you want to sell a will writing service. You want to then talk about all of the problems that can occur if you die without your your will done, and how much misery and problems that can cause, and how much money it's going to cost your family, and what a nightmare it's going to be and everybody in tears and all that sort of stuff. That's a great way to sell it.

You want to sell insurance. The best way to sell is talking about all the problems that happens if you don't get insured.

If you doing a comparison supermarket, talk about getting ripped off by other people.

Sorry, I'll stop there!

So E stands for easier or better life.

Better life is they want their life to be enhanced.

"L'Oreal, because you're worth it." It's about if you buy this, then your life will be enhanced. But it's not only about that. It's about the whole process of is it enhancing when you are buying something? How does it make your life easier or better.

For example, I recently had a problem with a car. My car is leased, and the car dealer had absolutely violated this principle, so much so that I'm thinking "I will never, never go to that dealer again, and I will tell everyone I know that they are a dealer to be avoided." They were all over me like a rash before I signed the paper, but now six months later I've got a problem that needs solving it's the buck passing

Olympics going on there. It's continual phone calls, and it's continual waiting. It's continual people saying, "You need to speak to so and so. It's not my problem, mate." I've made about four or five phone calls so far. So they've absolutely violated this principle, they've made my life harder and worse.

All they need to do was the first person I spoke to take ownership and say, "I'll take ownership of this and we'll work out a way to deal with it, and we'll come back to you." That's all that needed to happen, but there you are!

So E stands for Easy & Better, and

A stands for Attention.

Your customer wants to feel like you give a damn about them.

When I was doing a lot of work and training in pubs, one of the most important things is attention. When a customer comes through the door, make sure that someone is going to say hello to them and greet them within about five seconds – because that is the most important moment in the whole experience of the pub, that when they come through the door they actually feel like someone cares.

That's vitally important and how many businesses screw that one up in one way or another?

So:

- **Trust**
- **Easy Life**
- **Attention**

These three things apply to every business but in different formats.

So for example, going back to pubs. It's about attention as we've discussed, then about a better life. Every experience within that visit needs to be about making their life better. It's enhancing, it's a voluntary purchase. So it's enhancement, rather than easier. And trust is obviously important. They want to make sure that the food's sourced properly, the beer is well kept, the prices are fair, all that sort of stuff. But that definitely comes after the other two.

Let's go back to insurance. For insurance, it's definitely about E. First of all, making life easier and better. Absolutely, that's the key to insurance - and more or less all service companies, about making life easier. So many service companies mess this up because they think it's about how good they are at their job and what stuff they know. But it isn't! It's about making stuff easier for the customer.

With an accountant or a lawyer, it's about how they communicate with the customer. It's about how caring they are. So Easier first, then Trust, of course. Trust very close second because you've got to trust that this person is going to do the right job, and Attention, although it's in third place, it's absolutely vital. You need to make sure that people are getting the right attention. That's the area where most services, most professional businesses fall down. They're not giving the attention.

We can go for any business, but the mix is totally different in each situation.

So your your challenge here is first of all to learn the meaning of **TEA – TRUST, EASY OR BETTER LIFE** and **ATTENTION.** You've got the free resource. This can go on your 'could do' list, and it should be relatively easy.

Customers always want a cup of tea. Nice and easy to remember!

But then when you've done that, also look at your internal customers.

First of all, start with the people who are working with you who are making stuff work for your external customers. What mix of this tea will infuse and motivate them?

And then move to your external customers. What mix of tea will make them want to be enthused, motivated, loyal, spreading your reputation for all the right reasons and telling all their friends to come to you so when they come back and they rave about you?

What is the mix that they're going to need from that?

And lastly, how do these tea mixes change depending on the context or timing?

And then of course you need to work out how do you find that out? How do you know what the different contexts of your customer are? How do you know what your internal customers really want? How do you know what your external customers really want? That's what we're going to move on to in Principle No 4 about the measure, which is how to put proper feedback systems in place.

The key here is to put systems in place (step by step) that show the customer that you care, that demonstrate the attention through their execution – (I'll give you an example of this in a minute) – so that the customers want to be an ambassador, so that customers want to engage.

So a good example is a system I've put in many pubs now.

One of the pubs I invented this for was a pub in Somerset.

- When the person I was in partnership with took it over, it was taking under £700 a week. We engaged these '4 Vital Principles of Business Success' in this pub and put them into place, and the one that I want to talk to you about here is this one about how to engage the customer. How to find out the customer's real needs and how to put a measurement system in place - and also talk about that the customer focus mission. The point being that by doing this, the customers became our advocates, customers would tell us. We had a queue of people wanting to work for us. So internal customers absolutely got it. And from a pub that was taking under £700 a week, within a year it was taking over £14,000 a week. So it was over 20 times as busy just by doing the right thing. Okay, we refurbished it as well, of course, but it's absolutely about customer engagement.

Customers want to feel like they're engaged. They want to be engaged. They want to feel like you care. Even if it's buying the tiniest thing, they want to feel like there's something a little bit extra, the extra inch. So the smallest purchase is all about the tiny extra inches and how it's packaged, how it's delivered, how it's advertised, etc.

Recently I was buying an alarm clock. It cost me £11. I bought it from Amazon because the way that it was described on Amazon, I could see the information I really needed. Whereas another place I was looking at it gave the basic information, but they didn't explain it in detail and how it works. Amazon had a a little video of how it worked, all for £11. And of course with Amazon it's next day delivery. That's another extra inch. That's about an extra mile actually, but it's a series of extra inches that got them to that. And it's about the fact that you know that if anything goes wrong, you can immediately send it back in and there'll be no quibble.

- But going back to this pub. We settled on a customer focused mission of 'We want our customers to leave with a smile on their face, keen to return.' Great! How do we do that? Well, we need to make sure that we consider their emotional needs at every step. What do they need when they arrive in the car park? Well, it's got to be fantastically clean and tidy. All the plants have got to be blooming. There's got to be clear notices, etc, etc. So we put a system in place for that.

- What do they need when they come through the front door, or before they get to the front door? They've got to know what's available inside the pub so they know whether to come in or out, so they feel safe. So we put a system in place to make sure that was right.

- When they come into the pub, what's the first thing? They're going to need a fantastic greeting within five seconds. So we put a system like that in place, and every single step in the business.

- But the key thing I want to talk to you about here is the system we put in place for feedback. It's really hard to get feedback from people in a pub because you can't stop people and go, "Would you mind just telling me how you feel about your experience in this pub?" Or "Would you mind please filling this form in?" Or sending them an email afterwards, saying, "Please tell us your experience."

- There are lots and lots of businesses like this, and very often the first thing they hear about the customer's experience is when they get a review on Google or Trip Advisor or wherever it is. Google Review is massively influential now, so you've really got to get to grips of this and we will talk about this hugely in the fourth principle, the measure.

- 'What we did was we put a little box right at the front door, a transparent perspex box, and it said, "How was your experience today? Great, okay, or poor? And if you want to know all the theory behind this, you need to get hold of my book called "Great or Poor," which explains exactly all about this and how it works. We'll probably refer to this again. We offer a free information booklet 'How to Build a Feedback System that actually Works.' That should be available. You should be able to see that wherever you are to download that for free. If you can't find it, drop us a line we'll send it to you. It's completely free. There's no obligation.

- So – we had this box, How was your experience today? Great, okay, or poor?" When the person comes into the pub they get a friendly greeting and they get showed to the table. When they get to the table, the waiter or waitress comes to them and introduces themselves by name. They're wearing a T-shirt which has a big picture of a smiley cat on the front saying, "My job today is to make you look like this when you leave." A huge smiley cat" Everyone laughs. On the back it said, "If I have done so, please tell all your friends. But if I haven't done, please tell me or my manager before you leave." It makes it absolutely clear what we want from them in order to make sure that we can deliver fantastically for them.

- And then the waiter or waitress stands at the table and says, "Our job here is to make sure you have a fantastic time as it says on this stupid shirt I'm wearing. And on the back it says about if we do, please tell your friends that's what we do. We've got a card there for you. You can fill that in if you want to become part of our VIP Club, or if you want to send this information to your friends here's a whole load of stuff for that.

- But if there's anything wrong, please tell me before you leave. Please tell me at any time because I am here to make sure this happens. That is my job. That is what I'm paid to do. And if you don't feel comfortable telling me, my manager is over there. His name is Eddie. Please tell him before you leave, because our job is to make sure that we get this right. So hope you have a wonderful time. Is that clear? Any questions?"

- And then they hand over a poker chip saying, "Last thing, when you leave you'll have noticed a box at the front door. This is my poker chip. This is my colour." Each server had a different colour so we could hold each of them accountable to their colour. They were doing this a lot better than I'm describing it, by the way because I'm describing it fairly boringly, but they were trained to do this brilliantly, and they're much better at than I ever would be.

- So again, this poker chip is personalised to them. "So look, please, as I said to you, I am paid to make sure this happens. My role is to make sure you feel happy to put that in the great box on the way out. And if you don't, please tell us what we need to do in order to make sure that happens." I repeated that a bit, but it all went into one thing, and it was much more slick than I've done it – but can you see the point? The point is that it was a system set up to make the customer feel comfortable in telling us their real needs, and telling us what we needed to do in order to fulfil their real needs – making sure that it was very unlikely that they would leave with a bad reputation in their mouths ready to tell other people.

- So that was what caused this huge explosion. This thing grew by word of mouth massively. As I say, within a year it was taking 20 times as much money. We had a queue of people wanting to work for us. Literally, when we opened the doors at 12 o'clock at lunchtime, there was a queue of 20 to 30 people outside there every day wanting to come in. And that is no exaggeration, because I witnessed it myself.

Funnily enough, moving away from the pub now. Whenever I go into a company as a consultant, the first thing I do is find out what they want to achieve.

But the second thing I do is I spend time in the business, a day or a couple of days in the business, listening to people. What is their TEA? What matters to them? What what do they need to trust their business more, to trust their boss more, to want to be more engaged? What do they need to have an easier or a better life in their role?

What do they need to feel like someone cares about them, feel like they matter, in order so that they can then get on and make sure that they are delivering day in and day out like raving fans of their own business?

These are the key things that so few businesses do. There's so few that get it, but it makes your **TEA.**

It's your internal customers, what mix of **TEA** will enthuse and motivate them.

Your external customers, what mix of **TEA** will make them want to keep coming back buy more, and rave about you?

How do the **TEA** mixes change depending on context or timing?

A pub is another good example of this. Are they there for a romantic meal? In which case they'll have one type of **TEA** mix, or are they there for a business meeting? Totally different **TEA** mix.

You need to know all of these different contexts of why and how customers are coming to you, and then what are the **TEA** mixes for them.

We'll teach you a system in the next principle - the next principle is **Action: A** – the A of the BEAR – and the action is to **go the extra inch**.

We will teach you the inch by inch system, BUT the key here is to work out the **TEA** mixes for different customers, different scenarios, different contexts and then use these as a filter for every single system and process in your business.

Remember: Make sure you put systems and processes in your business one by one, little by little, step by step, to blow their socks off inch by inch, using simple systems.

So remember when I talked about the pub we had a system to make sure that all the signs were clean, the car park was beautiful, the flowers were alive, the boards were right, the information outside was right, the feedback system was right. Every one of those has a little tiny system behind it. It's not rocket science, but those systems evolved one by one.

➢ Let's just nail this system this week.

➤ Let's nail the next system next week.

➤ Let's nail the system after that the week after

It doesn't happen all at once. You nail it one by one because these systems need to last forever.

So there you are, the meaning of TEA. There's loads of stuff there for your 'could do' list.

Start by engaging your internal customers. Find out what their mix of TEA might be.

Then perhaps put some feedback systems in place (and wait till the end of this book to learn about feedback systems).

Send off for our free ebook 'How to Build a Feedback System that actually Works' before you start doing that. You can find it on our website: www.slow-selling.org or feel free to email us at support@slow-selling.org for your free copy with no strings attached.

Then start learning what makes them want to keep coming back and raving about you, little by little.

And then look at your different contexts, the **TEA** mixes.

So loads there for your 'could do' list. Absolutely vital to do, but do them one at a time, do them inch by inch, do them week by week, and we'll teach you how to do that.

So there you are. The second principle is E - Emotions, the customer's real needs, and to find those out and to use those as a filter for every system and process step by step in your business.

'Customers' REAL Needs'

Learn the meaning of 'TEA'

• Internal customers: what mix of TEA will enthuse and motivate them?

• External customers: what mix of TEA will make them want to keep coming back, buy more and rave about you?

• How do these TEA mixes change depending on context or timing?

• How do you find out?

RECAP

Okay, now we've done the first two principles, and now it's time for a brief recap on what we've covered so far. So let's just keep this fresh so we can all remember what's going on.

The first thing we discussed was the idea of the background - the background to the market, the fact that as a small business the key is to focus on customer loyalty, reputation and referrals. That can be your unique selling point.

In fact, that's the only way to out compete your bigger and better funded competition. That's the only way to make a true impact and to make really great progress in any small business without resorting to special offers and bribes and really getting yourself in a muddle and in deep water.

The second thing we talked about was the idea of principles.

Principles drive everything. The idea that in order to really compete in the area of customer loyalty, reputation and referrals, you need, of course, to have systems making that happen.

It doesn't happen by luck. Luck is not a system. Luck is not a strategy. In order to do this, **you have to have systems.**

So therefore, what sort of systems do you need?

Well, you need systems that are based on common sense. Timeless principles of universal common sense, as I say, and you need these systems to be simple and easy to apply, step by step, in any small business no matter how small it is, no matter how big it is. You're busy, you don't want extra hassle. You need these things to be easy to apply, and you need them to be based on clearly understandable, simple, common sense principles.

Then we talked about the principles of human behaviour. We talked about the fact that people behave like bears, people have beliefs that drive their emotions, that cause their actions, that give them results.

Therefore in order to get everyone in every system in your business behaving effectively so that you can build your business through reputation, loyalty and referrals, you need to make sure that every single person, every single process, every single system in your business is driven by these four principles.

We've covered the first two principles:

The first principle being B – Beliefs. The need for your business to have this compass. This customer focused mission being the compass for everything that you do.

The second principle being E – Emotions. To understand your customers' real needs - the cup of **TEA: TRUST, EASIER or BETTER LIFE**, and **ATTENTION.** Understand those, and look in your business at every step, in every process, in every circumstance, what is that mix and how are you going to deliver them?

Now we move onto the second two timeless, universal common sense principles, the BEAR principles.

The third one is ACTIONS.

What are the actions you're going to need to take?

We're going to talk here about **going the extra inch**. We're going to talk about that in a minute and then after that we'll talk about the R of the BEAR – the RESULTS. In order to get great results, you need to have great measures because what gets measured gets done. We're going to talk about what measures you need to put in place to make sure all of these things that we're discussing actually happen.

So without any further ado, let's move on to Principle No 3 – A for ACTION. Go the extra inch.

PRINCIPLE NO 3: ACTION

Principle No 3 of the '4 VITAL PRINCIPLES OF BUSINESS SUCCESS' is the ACTION planning, the ACTION, process, the ACTION step. The ACTION is to take is to go the extra inch. **To slow down and go the extra inch.**

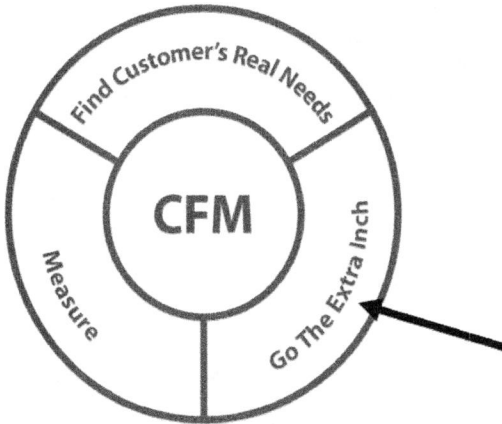

The whole purpose of this idea of 'going the extra inch' is to **slow down and take things in small steps.**

Why do you want to slow down and take things in small steps? It's because small steps are achievable, motivational and sustainable.

A great example of this is the 'Aggregation of Marginal Gains.'

Look at the British Cycling Team and how they went from being one of the worst teams in the world to the best in the world.

The 'Aggregation of Marginal Gains': Continual inches, continuous small steps, practised weekly, monthly, quarterly, annually, over time will make you amazing, and it will keep you amazing if you keep going forward.

Positive: the aggregation of marginal gains

1% better every day 1.01^{365} = 31.18

1% worse every day 0.99^{365} = 0.03

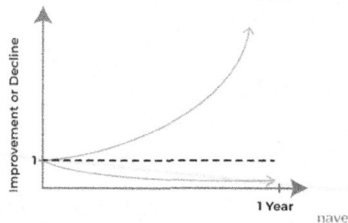

Improvement or Decline

1 Year

nave

Of course, as soon as you think you're there, as soon as you think you've achieved excellence, you've got to where you want to get to, that's the time when you want to keep going because others are trying to catch you.

If you're on top of your game, someone else is trying to put you out all the time. As soon as any business stops trying to improve, that's when of course they start getting into real trouble.

I think the best example of this in the UK in recent years – (or not actually that recent anymore), was Marks & Spencer. When I was about 20, Marks & Spencer was the third biggest retailer in the world. Now they're not even the third biggest retailer in the UK, nowhere near. This is because they stopped trying to improve. They got to this amazing stage where they were really, really good, and then they stopped continually improving and of course everyone suddenly overtook them.

Once you've been overtaken, once you've been made to look a bit silly, once you look a bit like yesterday's news, it's almost impossible to turn that round and get back to where you need to be.

So this continual process of small steps:

✓ If you're a startup, what is the first small step you need to take to start making sure that the key business driver is going to be customer loyalty, reputation, and hopefully referrals?

✓ If you are a small business just got going, what are the small steps you need to start developing to do that?

✓ If you are moving from a one-man band to employing someone, what are the small steps you need to start with?

✓ If you are running your own business and perhaps working part time to pay the bills - and there's lots of people doing that - what small steps do you need to take to develop your small business so that you can have the confidence to give that part time job up and plunge directly into being full time self-employed, having your own business?

✓ If you are a small business with one or two staff, what small steps do you need to take to start moving and growing and employing more people?

What are all these small steps?

Of course there's a multitude of small steps that need to be taken and I write about them extensively in my books: 'Great or Poor' and 'Slow Selling.' So please do have a look at those books.

We teach all the time about how to do this through our 'Effective use of time', our 'Effective communication', our 'Slow selling for business leaders', and our 'Slow selling to internal customers' (we call employees internal customers) training programmes.

So there's lots and lots of material we have for that, but the principle here is to slow down and look at going the extra inch. Going the extra inch on a weekly basis. Going the extra inch on a monthly basis. Going the extra inch on a quarterly basis. Going the extra inch on an annual basis:

Continual, continual, continual, and building, building, building one step on each other.

As Lao-Tzu famously said, *"A journey of a thousand miles starts with the first step."*

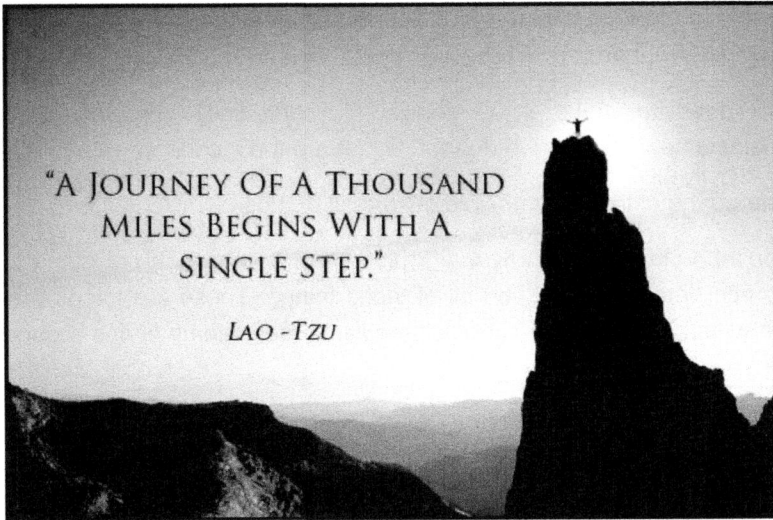

> "A JOURNEY OF A THOUSAND MILES BEGINS WITH A SINGLE STEP."
>
> *LAO-TZU*

This is going the extra inch on **systems** to build up new systems.

This is going the extra inch on **processes** to make sure that the processes are just getting inch by inch better and better.

This is going the extra inch on **strategy**. What is changing in the market, and what do we need to start developing inch by inch? What do we need to be changing and innovating, growing and doing?

And going the extra inch on **behaviour**, how can we make sure that our behaviour is continually improving, and everyone across the business is demonstrating the top possible level of behaviour? How can we be continually going the extra inch on customer expectations? How can we continually over-deliver just by a tiny bit that is continually sustainable?

And going the extra inch on **measures**: What are working? What are helpful? What aren't? What else might we need?

We need to make it all consistent, continually improving and sustainable. How can we do that? What are the inches we need?

The go the extra inch principle covers all of those.

You'll be pleased to know that in this short book, we're not going to go into details and tell you all of those things. Those are things that we write about in all of our other areas. There's plenty of tips around for you.

A particularly good book in this area is one called 'The E-Myth.'

Another is a fantastic book by Julian Richer, Head of Richer Sounds – 'The Richer Way.'

There's 'Business Think' by Covey.

There is 'The 7 Habits of Highly Effective Managers.' That's another great one. There's 'Management in 10 Words' by Terry Leahy.

'The 4 Disciplines of Education,' another Covey book.

There's lots and lots of material here. You can study this material inch by inch, but you can also find your extra inches by using small, easy to apply systems and tools based on principles of common sense - and that's exactly what we're going to talk about now.

So the idea of go the extra inch is to look at every step of your customer journey, and go the extra inch steps into all systems, processes and behaviours.

Then to put daily, weekly, monthly go the extra inch systems in place as well.

We're going to talk about that, but daily go the extra inch systems may be a daily huddle. May be a daily focus on one thing you can change today.

I publish a journal which is called the 'Go the Extra Inch Journal.' So have a look at my website for that. Each journal will take you over 26 weeks on a weekly and daily basis of continual extra inches.

On a weekly basis we'll talk about the weekly compass, and we'll talk about the team 'go the extra inch process', and on a monthly basis looking at strategy, and about how the market's moving.

It's definitely about gathering and reviewing feedback, of course.

Maybe it's about the customer journey. We can track customers through a particular journey.

So 'Go the extra inch' is all about putting systems in place in all these ways.

We're going to talk about three simple systems, but before we talk about them, the question is where do the inches come from? Where can those inches come from?

'Go the extra inch'

- Look at every step of the customer journey
- Put 'Go the extra inch' steps into all systems, processes and behaviours.
- Put daily, weekly and monthly 'Go the extra inch' systems in place

- Where do the 'inches' come from?

Now, I've hope you've said to yourself:

- "Those inches are going to come from customer feedback."

Remember, this is not about customer service. **This is about customer experience.**

The customer doesn't care a damn about your service. They don't care what you think you're doing. They don't care how many consultants you've spoken to. They don't care how many books you've read. They don't care how many really cool systems you've put in place. They don't care about all that old marketing and promotions old stuff that everyone's going to try and get you to buy.

What they care about is their experience, **how they feel about it, how they feel treated, how they were attracted to you, how they became interested in you, what caused them to be converted to use you, what was their experience of using you? What did they**

think after they used you, and what are they going to do in the future?

So it's all about customer feedback and customer experience, and using that to powerfully generate continual extra inches through systems.

As Terry Leahy said, remember, *"It's all about listening to the customer, and doing what they said we should do. It's all free advice. All we've got to do is listen to it and put it into practice."*

We will talk about this a lot more shortly in Principle No 4, which is 'measure'.

So we're suggesting to you that the information for the extra inches comes from the expert in your business, which is the customer.

That can be the customer external, of course, but it can also be the internal customer - those people who are working for you and with you. It can be suppliers, it can be community, it can be anybody who cares for you, any stakeholder who has an interest in your success.

So what are those three tools that we're going to talk about?

Well, the first tool is called the **weekly compass plan**.

This is a weekly, 'get off the bus, get out of the whirlwind,' and to work on your business, on yourself, on your teams, on your goals, on your processes. It's the weekly compass plan. I'm not going to talk to you about it at all here because you need to go to our website.

We have lots of free resources on this, which explains to you how a weekly compass plan works, what it looks like, how to do it. All the resources are there on the website: www.Slow-Selling.org. They're all there, they're all free. You can download them, and that's exactly where you are.

All I'm saying here is that to go the extra inch, the weekly compass plan is an absolutely key tool. In fact, with any training that I do, I say to people,

"The key thing that you need to be using is this weekly compass plan because it gives you the opportunity to get out of the whirlwind, to step off the bus, and work on your business, on your team, on your projects, on your goals, whatever it is, little by little, step by step.

And then to put those plans back into your business, schedule them and put them in as appointments that are not to be disturbed so that you can then, go ahead and get on with it."

All these three tools are themselves a free download. We are making these tools free on our website..

ACTION: go to www.slow-selling.org/resources and download the free tools

And of course, if you want more information come to us. We'll send you free information, or we'll suggest ways that we can coach you, help you, work with you, whatever is suitable for your needs.

The second tool is called the **customer journey template**.

This is a simple little spreadsheet that you can adapt to your particular circumstances, which looks at your customer journey the whole way through:

- from awareness to consideration,
- to whatever decisions they need to make,

- to whatever services they get,

- to the use of your product or service,

- to the after sales, the after use,

- and to the reputation and loyalty following all of that.

It takes you through all of those stages, and it works through the customer focus mission: the customers' goal, the moments of truth, the customers' real needs, the **Trust, Easier or Better Life**, and **Attention.**

What extra inches can you put into those steps?

(And for the measure: How are you going to measure the success and the execution of those steps, and then some other key things like what's the KPI in your business? Who's responsible? What's the system? And then what extra inch can your system go? How can your system go an extra inch at every step to make sure your customer comes away from you and goes, "Fantastic! They are absolutely amazing. I can't wait to deal with them again.")

That is absolutely the key to it, **to work on every step of your customer journey, every moment of truth in your customers' interaction with you, step by step, little by little, inch by inch, week by week**.

Work on it, work on it, work on it **one step at a time**, and you will get better and better and better.

And over time you will become world class with customers who absolutely love you, who can't wait to buy from you again, who tell all their friends about you, and buy as much as they can from you. That is the holy grail.

The third go the extra inch tool is called the '**go the extra inch process**'.

It's a process to help you motivate teams, to get them working together to go the extra inch as teams.

It's about creating a cycle of continual action through clear and compelling lead measures – measures of what matters to the customer at every step and interaction. It's each person in the team doing five things each week as a team process to:

1. Account for the actions they promised last time.

2. Identify something done well by others, something they've noticed from somewhere else. It's a sharing of best practice. It's gathering good information.

3. Identifying an area for development in themselves or in their team.

4. Committing to an extra inch in that.

5. Identifying the help they need from others in the team to do it.

So it's a cycle of continual action. It's a high impact process to help you continually develop and work on this as a team.

Again, I'm not going into that one in detail either because there is free information on the website: Slow-Selling.org. There's free guidance on that about how to do it, and if you need any help, you want someone to come into your team and run a guided go the extra inch process so you can then take it forward and do it for yourself forevermore, then of course you know who to contact.

So that's what it's all about.

The three tools:

- The weekly compass plan.
- The customer journey template, moving you forward inch by inch in your systems.
- The go the extra inch process for team continual improvement and development.

There are of course many different tools that can be used, and we discuss them in our books 'Great or Poor' and 'Slow Selling' … these are just 3 key starters that can lead you on, step by step, to other 'go the extra inch' tools, processes and behaviours.

So there you have it: Go the extra inch – the key of continual improvement in small steps that's achievable, realistic, and if kept up over the long term will turn you from just about okay, to:

"Fantastic! We love you, we want to buy as much from you, we can't wait to come back to you, and we're going to tell all our friends to use you."

That is how it's done: the key is to go the extra inch.

PRINCIPLE NO 4: RESULTS

So moving on with the '4 Vital Principles of Business Success,' we now move to the Principle No 4 – The R of the BEAR principles:

Beliefs: Emotions: Actions: Results

The R is Results, so **Principle No 4 is 'Results'**.

What we're suggesting here is that you need to **slow down and measure what matters.**

This is about considering measures of cause versus measures of effect.

Every business – (apart from a few completely nightmare ones) has measures of effect, ie, how many customers, how much money, how many sales, how many costs, how much advertising, promotional costs? The figures that your accountant gets from you, and your accountant produces for the tax man. These are measures of effect. These are measures of things that have happened. These are measures of outputs.

Now these are very interesting to accountants, but they do not help you in running your business.

You cannot say "I'm going to learn how to run my business better next year because of my current sales in the current quarter - the marketing cost versus customer income." It's just too slow. It's too blunt.

They can give you some help, some guidance, but in order to help you run a business and continually find ways to go the extra inch so that you could alter, develop, change, improve based on the customer's real needs - (Remember cup of tea – **TRUST, EASIER LIFE** and **ATTENTION)**, and to keep aligned with your customer focus mission, you need better measures.

Because using the output measures to run your business is like trying to drive your car only using the rear view mirror.

And I often tell this story.

- What would happen if your accountant treated your measures of effect, your measures of money or measures of output, in the same way that most businesses treat the measures of cause, ie, the actions, the behaviours that caused those effects?

- If they did, they would come to you and say: "Well, I think your business is sort of alright. I can see that you've got too many bounced cheques. You haven't told me that the bank manager's been pestering you on the phone. I think most of the direct debits have gone through, and I think that most of the customers have paid. I hope they have because they sort of like us."

Yet that is the way that people are running their business - from the point of view of the cause of the effects!

We need measures of the cause!

We need what we call a business barometer to tell us what their customer behaviour is likely to be tomorrow rather than a weather report, (which is like your P&L) which tells us what the customer behaviour was yesterday.

- We need to know what the customer behaviour is going to be.

- We need to know what our people's behaviour is going to be.

- We need to know what's going to make people more loyal to us.

- We need to know what is going to make people want to rave about us behind our back.

- We need to know what is going to make people want to refer us,

- and we need to know what are the inches that we need to employ across our business to continually improve and go the extra inch across our systems, and our processes, and our behaviour, and our people and all that sort of stuff.

We need this stuff. It's absolutely vital, yet so few businesses have it.

This is a huge opportunity for you because **if you can put this in place in your business, you can at a stroke be so much better than the vast majority of your competition.**

A barometer is so much more useful than a weather report.. It's so much more helpful to you in deciding what clothes to wear and what behaviour you're going to adopt during the day, than the report of what the weather did yesterday or last month!

So please, please please from today, don't try and run your business only with weather reports of what happened yesterday, what happened last week, and what happened last month - because what gets measured gets done.

You need the right measures. You need to understand the difference between measures of cause and measures of result.

Measures of cause are the measures of what will cause a result.

We call these 'lead measures.' Measures that are going to lead you, lead your people, lead your behaviour, lead your systems down the right routes continually, extra inch by inch to improve and therefore develop customer loyalty, reputation and referrals.

The measures of results will take care of themselves.

You don't need to worry about them. Your accountant will do them. Your administrator will do them. They take care of themselves, and **they will improve if you focus well on the measures of cause and you execute well on the measures of cause, inch by inch.**

As we said in the customer focus mission, we are not here to make money. That's a result. Remember, that's an output!

What are we here for?

We are here to do the right things so well – that's in input - **that the money will follow, not the other way around**. We are not here to make money. We are here to do the right thing so well so that customers love us, want to come back to us, want to rave about us to their friends so that the money will then follow, not the other way around. It's absolutely vital. It's easy to say, bloody hard to apply. So few businesses apply this well, and one of the key pieces to start applying this, of course is with your measures -because what gets measured gets done. So the key is to start measuring the measures of cause.

So what are the measures of cause? What can we measure? What can we do? The No 1 is customer feedback. And I don't mean here, naff, cheap, off the shelf systems that someone else has invented and you can download for next to nothing. You can do this sort of stuff and get a few stars here and there, have a bit of a click on a website and make the odd email. Those are naff. They tell you nothing. They give you terrible feedback. They give you misleading feedback. They give you false confidence. They are fit for the bin only.

This is totally turning your business the other way round so that customer feedback becomes the driver of everything you do. The aim to do the right thing, to do things as well as possible, becomes the driver of everything you do as you set out in your customer focus mission. You actually hold yourself accountable and ask the customer to hold yourself accountable.

And as I said right from the start, we give the example of this operating in the pub that we ran and where we tested out all these ideas. At the doorway into the pub was this big plastic box saying, "How was your experience today: Great, okay or poor?" All members of staff were trained in this and their job descriptions were changed. They were now no longer bar people, waiters or waitresses, or cleaning people or cooking people or whatever. Everyone had the same job. Everyone's job was to make sure that the customer left with a smile on their face keen to return. Every system in the business started with those words. *'The purpose of this system is to ensure that the customer leaves with a smile on their face, keen to return.'* Every process was put in place with that as the driver, the mission. And then of course it was developed using the customer's real needs as the guidance, the filter, and developed inch by inch, gathering feedback along the way to help move those inches forward.

Everyone had a T-shirt on. On the front of which was a smiley cat saying, *"My job is to make you look like this today."* And on the back it said, *"If I do, please tell all your friends. And if I don't, please tell me or my manager before you leave."*

If you want a copy of that – you want a picture of those shirts – please contact us. We can send you in the right direction for that.

Then they also had the poker chips. They had cards on the table explaining about this. They had to explain to every single person what this was about, what they were there for, and that they wanted to make sure that this person wanted to put their poker chip in the 'great' slot on the way out. And if they couldn't, please convey that and let them know before they left, to give them a chance to change their mind and move it up to 'great' by doing all the right things.

So it's about a whole system. It's a whole system - absolutely generating this positive, proactive, in your face. In your face works very well in the pub situation. It might not be so good in other situations. I do understand that. We've done this for solicitors, we've done this for accountants, we've done this for other professional advisors, we've done this for IT companies, we've done this for hotels, we've of course done it for a lot of pubs. We've done it for recruitment companies, done it for estate agents, we've done it for letting companies, we've done it for wholesalers, we've done it for manufacturers, we've done it for parts suppliers. We've done it for one-man bands, we've done it for major international corporations. It absolutely works and you've got to get it right each time.

Now, let me point you at this stage to another free resource that we offer here. It's offered by our sister company – Investors in Feedback. This free resource is, as usual, on our website: Slow-Selling.org. It's about delivering, putting together, measuring and accrediting feedback systems for businesses. It's a free a free resource and it's called 'How to Build a Feedback System that actually Works.' It's a free ebook. It's about 30 pages, but it's absolutely stuffed full of information to make sure that you don't make the mistake of putting some naff, half-arsed, half-witted feedback system in place. Then you say to me, "Well, we tried the feedback system. It didn't bloody work." Well, of course it won't work if you don't put the right system in place.

If you believe what I'm saying here – you may not, that's fine - but if you do believe what I'm saying, then please, please, please trust me on this. You absolutely have to put the right feedback system in place. It needs to be driven by your customer focus mission, filtered through the customer's real needs, put together inch by inch so it actually works – so that your customer actually wants to tell *you* before anyone else, so that your customer becomes your partner, your advocate, a raving fan, so that they become part of the whole process and together you build this amazing thing.

So customer feedback systems: Go to the website, download that free ebook 'How To build a Feedback System that Actually Works.' There's a whole lot more information on this because customer feedback is the most powerful information you can get. It is a great lead measure, but it's usually messed up, and you need to make sure that it's done at the right time, using the right method in the right way, driven by the right people with the right process and the right tools, and the right follow up. So there's a lot of things you can get wrong here.

Everyone thinks customer feedback is easy. "Well you just download some system off the web and it'll cost a few quid each month." No, no, no. Please don't do that. Please spend time on this. Do it inch by inch. Slow down. The process we call 'Slow Selling. Slowing down to do this right.

And a reminder of the words of Terry Leahy again: *"The customer gives the leadership of the business the plain and simple truth about the business, and it's the most honest feedback you ever get."*

In my experience, if you listen really closely, they not only tell you what's wrong, but they actually tell you what you need to do, and it's all free advice. Then what you need to have to do is believe them and act on it.

So there you have it! The idea of having measures. Measures of cause rather than measures of effect, and the No 1 measure being customer feedback.

There are of course other measures that you can use as well, but they must be used in conjunction with customer feedback. Things like:

- Customer effort score: how difficult or easy it is for the customer to deal with you.
- Loyalty score. How loyal are people to you, and what for?

- Transfer rate. How easy is it for a customer to get around your business and then to deal with you?

- Referral score. How many referrals do you get? What percentage of your new customers come from referrals?

- Recruitment score. How easy is it to recruit someone? That's a fantastic measure of a business.

Whenever we deal with businesses, one of the key things we talk about is how can we make sure that people start queuing up to work for your business – because that is a fantastic measure of the success, the popularity, and how wonderful your business is. How far are people queuing up?

Going back to this pub that we talked about, we had a queue of at least 15 people waiting to work for us at any one time. People used to say, "I'd really like to know if you've got any jobs going. Please, can you put me on your list if you have anything going?"

Another score we can do is customer lifetime value. What is the value of a customer of a lifetime? That's a massively important score? How much will that affect how people deal with you?

In the pub we measured tips, and we incentivised people on tips. We told customers about tips and why we incentivised them and where the tips went. So tips is another another measure, but you can put lots and lots of different lead measures in place in your business. And of course, this free download 'How to Build a Feedback System that Actually Works,' goes into detail on all of these, and it will give you everything you need to know. So please do go to our website and download that.

So there you are! You have measure. That's the R – the R of BEAR, the measure. You need to have the right measures in place. There need to be measures of cause that is going to help you run your business better to go the extra inch in alignment with your customer focus mission, and filtering every single step through your three vital customers real needs.

WHAT ARE YOU GOING TO DO NEXT?

So there we have it. Those are the '4 Vital Principles of Business Success,' and we've just got one more thing where we're going to round this up and tell you what you can do next.

So that is the '4 Vital Principles of Business Success.'

You need to have:

- Principles.
- Systems
- Continuous and Continual Improvement
- Step by Step.

So the key to success is simple systems. Whether you are thinking of a startup, you're a one person band, you're looking to recruit to your first person or your third, fourth, fifth, tenth, twentieth person or more, the key is always the same. Simple systems driven by these timeless, universal common sense principles to deliver consistency and continual improvement in the customer experience, step by step so that customers want to be continually more loyal to you. They want to spread your reputation around the world, they want to tell others to come to you, and they want to refer people to you.

That is the key. That is the one thing you can do better than anything else, and this is the system that will enable you to do it.

So the question then, of course, is what are you going to do next?

It doesn't matter whether you like it. It doesn't matter what you think of it. It is just principles. And it doesn't matter whether you buy anything from us or not. What matters is that you actually do something different in your business, in your life, from having read this.

So here is a simple checklist of things that you could do. Some of the things are paid for. Some of the things are free. There's no there's no pressure to buy anything. It's absolutely up to you to do what is right for you, in your situation, in your business. And remember, that we are a not for profit philanthropic organisation. I've learnt these principles through hard work and study over my whole professional career where my focus has been on turning businesses into world class businesses.

Everything on our 'Slow Selling website, our Slow Selling movement, is focused on empowering small businesses, and helping small business owners by giving you the information, the tools, and the systems that is normally only available to big businesses. I've been taught this stuff. I've worked for FTSE 100 businesses. I've been there when this information has been imparted. I continually study it all my life. I've made enough money in my life. I don't need to keep on pushing and pushing and pushing. I'm here to try and share for philanthropic genuine reasons.

For those reasons everything that we do we aim to be never expensive, and always easy to access, and everything we do is also guaranteed. We have this very simple, no nonsense guarantee. If you don't like what we've done, tell us and we'll put it right. If you still don't like it, we'd only ever expect you to pay what you felt it was worth. It's that simple.

And of course, one more thing. If you liked this, please share it with friends. Please share it with other people who run businesses. As I say, there's no obligation to buy anything. There's lots and lots of free information at Slow Selling, and then there are further paid resources if you want to take it further.

So here is the list of what you can do going forward:

1. Make sure that you sign up to our mailing list - not because we want to try and sell you stuff, but because we will send you out on an infrequent basis, genuinely helpful information, links to new resources and ideas. The resources may be ours or from others, etc. We will just send them out to you if we would like to receive them ourselves. It's absolutely aligned with our philanthropic basis. It is *not* a way of getting you to sign up to something so we can bombard you with emails like, "Sign this now, a special offer for January! It's only this, it's only that. First 100 customers get it at this price." Definitely you won't get that rubbish. It's just about sending you helpful stuff.

2. Go to our website: Slow-Selling.org. Find the resources page and download and study the free resources there. In particular, of course, get that free ebook, 'How to Build a Feedback System that Actually Works.' There's lots and lots of value in that. And then you can use this with that ebook. You can work from those and you can certainly get a long way down the road with those.

3. The next thing we suggest you do is ridiculously cheap. It's just £7, because we want to make sure that people do it. We don't do it for free, because this is something where you need to

actually take some action. So that's why we charge a little bit for it. If you've paid that little tiny £7 - which we absolutely hope is not going to break your bank - subconsciously, you'll have paid something and you'll need to do it. It's called 'The Starter 4 10.' You should see lots and lots of links to this. It's on our website. You should have had stuff emailed to you. If you haven't for some reason because our system hasn't done what it should do, then the website is Starter410.org.

So go there and sign on. It's just £7. It's a seven week guided training, one little step at a time in 10 minutes a day. It comes to you by email, so it's really easy. You don't have to do anything. You just sign on and everything else will just happen. It just takes you through this these ideas, little by little, step by step in 10 minutes a day. It's absolutely applying the go the extra inch principle to get you started, to get you going, to give you that ability to take action. So I really strongly recommend that one. Starter410.org and sign up for that.

4. If you like that, and you want to develop more, of course we can then offer personal support. The best way to start personal support is by booking a two hour, one to one session by phone, or Zoom, (or whatever system you want to use) to listen to you to find out what's going on in your business, to see where you are and to help you start down the road with the right inches.

Now, we don't do what other people do, which is have this half an hour fact finding session for free. We don't do any of that old rubbish. The reason why we don't do that is because it's not helpful. It's completely dysfunctional.

The key is to spend two hours on this and do it really, really well, and let's just charge you a flat fee. At the time of writing this, the flat fee is £100 for two hours' work, which is about a third of our normal rate when we're working with companies. It might have gone up by the time you're reading this because I've no idea when you're going to be reading this – because there's lots of inflation around at the moment. But it will always be a flat fee. It will always be simple. It'll always be clear, and you will absolutely get massive value from this.

It's about two hours to really listen to you, find out what are your hopes, fears and goals in your life and in your business, and then start directing you down the right inches to start making all this stuff work for you. Absolutely vital! You can use that to maybe focus on a customer focus mission. You can use that to put a go the extra inch system in place. You can use that to start thinking about how to build a feedback system that really works for you, etc. So use it for what works for you - or you could use it just as a general chit chat to help point you in the right direction. Any of those things absolutely will work for you, so strongly recommend that as well.

5. Then when you've done all of that, of course you can then carry on with more personal, more in depth coaching and training, etc, We will tailor a situation that works for you. And although we do have a set rate for what we do, we generally offer a 'pay what you feel you can afford' system. We'll talk about that. Tell us what you feel comfortable with affording, and we'll see what we can do for you.

6. And lastly, if you are a coach or a trainer, then you can licence this material in order to use with your customers. But please, please, please don't use this unlicensed. The reason for that is not because we want to get loads of money for you. As I say, we

are a not for profit, philanthropic, focused on empowering and helping people. We will charge you a licence fee, but it will always be a not expensive fee.

The reason is that we need to make sure that we know who's licenced. We need to make sure that you stay up to date, you have all the right information, that you are trained in the right way, and the quality is maintained for customers. So it's absolutely in your interest as well as well as ours to make sure that happens.

So there you have it! There's free information. Sign up, download the free resources, absolutely make sure you sign up for the Starter 410. Probably a good idea to go for the two hour support at a fixed rate, and then you'll know where you are and what you want to do next – because then there's more in depth information available. There's other paid for resources on our website. It's absolutely up to you. Keep in contact with us, and we will find ways to help you and work with you.

Thanks very, very much for reading the '4 Vital Principles of Business Success.' Every absolute luck with your business! It's really tough to run a business out there. I personally have run many businesses. Some of them have been wildly successful. Some of them have been disastrous. I've also worked for other businesses. I've worked for FTSE 100 business, etc. Again, that doesn't really matter - apart from the fact to know that I've been there. I've been on the edge of despair. I've had breakdowns. I've been weeks from bankruptcy. I've obviously had some successes as well. So I know what it's like. I know how hard it is. So please do try and put some of these ideas into into place in your business. I'm sure they will help you.

As I say, "Every Inch Helps, and as Tesco says, "Every Little Helps!

So thank you very much again for taking the time out, and I absolutely hope this does fantastic things for you. Very good luck to you. Please do keep in contact.

The '4 Vital Principles of Business Success,' written by Guy Arnold.

Find out more at Slow-Selling.org

Printed in Great Britain
by Amazon